THE WARRIOR MINDSET

Francis Hoover

CHAPTER 1

PRESENTING THE HERO OUTLOOK

How to get a bulletproof mindset of fearless warrior

THE WARRIOR MINDSET

Francis Hoover

CHAPTER 1
Presenting the Hero Outlook

Have you at any point felt like life is a struggle? Like it can once in a while be a battle to get up in the first part of the day and do everything that you need to do? Do you ever wake up feeling continually drained and pushed? Does life simply appear excessively? Certainly, I get it. You have loads of work to do. You have obligation perhaps. Perhaps you're worn out from shopping and perhaps you have a stomach hurt.

Presently ponder a genuine fighter.

Ponder somebody who dozes harsh, uncertain of whether they're going kick the bucket during the evening. Then, at that point, they awaken, no time for a shower or a decent breakfast, and they jump straight into it. They overlook their injuries, they take lives and they see their companions and their faithful comrades shot and killed before them. In any case, no I get it. You're worn out. You needed to work until 6pm last evening...

What I'm getting at, is that your life isn't exactly hard. You could believe it's hard and now and then it could feel hard.

Yet, there are individuals out there with much more terrible lives than you. There are individuals out there who live with devastating ailment and not two pennies to rub together. Furthermore, a large number of them do this with a pride, an effortlessness and a courage that humiliates most of us.

The fighter mentality doesn't really have anything to do with battle. Truth be told, the evildoers that start bar brawls and that believe they're 'hard' for beginning quarrels are over as distant from genuine fighters as it gets. Ask any individual who has seen genuine battle if they would need to take a chance with their wellbeing and waste their energy on trying too hard to find something.

The champion mentality is unique. This is tied in with understanding what you need and making it work. It's tied in with being hard and it's about not allowing easily overlooked details to get you down. It's tied in with pushing ahead with what you know is correct and it's tied in with conveying liability and difficulty on your shoulders with poise and pride. It's about not allowing your feelings to get the better of you and it's about not taking the simple response or the simple course to tackle your concerns.

What is the Fighter Mentality?

The champion attitude is unique. This is tied in with understanding what you need and making it work. It's tied in with being hard and it's about not allowing easily overlooked details to get you down. It's tied in with pushing ahead with what you know is correct and it's tied in with conveying liability and

difficulty on your shoulders with respect and pride. It's about not allowing your feelings to get the better of you and it's about not taking the simple response or the simple course to tackle your concerns.

So where does this title and this move toward come from? What is the hypothesis behind the champion's mentality?

Obviously, it comes from our heartfelt picture of the fighter and from accounts of heroes from history. It comes from stories of our boldest people who faced genuine conflicts while staying even tempered, forfeiting themselves for other people and doing fantastic things.

Presently, we as a whole realize that truly, few out of every odd fighter fits this shape. For each gallant person who put themselves in the line of fire, there would have been hundreds additional warriors that whined, that were in it for some unacceptable reasons, or that wouldn't put themselves out for other people. Romanticizing fighting is as a matter of fact a horrendous thought - it is a genuinely terrible situation and not many individuals feel like 'champions' when they are confronted with foe fire.

However, that picture of the ideal 'hero' we're checking here out. Furthermore, at our ideas of history's most prominent fighters like the samurai or the Spartans.

The fact is that certain individuals figure out how to remain cool and quiet in even the most awful circumstances. Certain individuals continually move forward and don't permit little bothers or an absence of common luxuries hinder them.

What's more, those individuals shut us down. Those individuals submit our questions appear to be exceptionally very minor.

Presently suppose you could take that equivalent attitude and apply it to current life. Rather than getting worn out or stalled, rather than being diverted and enticed, you would rather drive forward with a relentless, impenetrable mindset. Your foes would shudder realizing that there was no way to stop you and your vocation obstructions, relationship objectives and monetary plans would all disintegrate underneath your will.

In the event that you apply an iron will and champion mindset to a cutting edge way of life, you get outrageous productivity, assurance and pride. Self-control, assurance and independence are characteristics that cause serious areas of strength for us that assist us with getting what we need. They are qualities that make us great guardians, old buddies and great accomplices. They are qualities that assist us with living with ourselves and to gain appreciation and adoration from others.

Suppose you had the psychological solidarity to sit in a freezing cold shower for a really long time. Suppose you weren't progressively eased in hazardous circumstances. Take those qualities and afterward put them facing the totally measly difficulties that the greater part of us face today. They would fall like dominos.

Having a champion's mentality and carrying on with current life is like swelling with muscles and lifting 5kg. Fostering that champion's mentality resembles an exercise for your brain, your way of thinking and your spirit.

It will make you relentless.

CHAPTER 2

The Point - The stuff to be a Hero

All in all, what are the occupants of the fighter mentality? What words could we at any point use to depict the advanced champion? Here are only a couple:

- Gutsy

- Self-Restrained

- Principled

- Solid willed

- Kind

- Development situated

- Independence

- Defensive

- Benevolent

- Quiet

- Dependable

- Persuasive, Motivating, Alluring

- Honorable

- Strong

- Unassuming (however not be guaranteed to humble)

These are only a portion of the characteristics that a genuine hero ought to take a stab at. These are a portion of the things we will be hoping to develop and better comprehend all through this book.

One more extraordinary portrayal of a champion comes from a far-fetched source: the Disney film Mulan. These statements are from the tune 'I'll Make a Man Out of You' yet as a matter of fact they can apply similarly to a lady.

Gracious, and in the event that you would rather not gain illustrations on valor from a Disney film, consider the way that Jackie Chan sang the Chinese variant of the tune. He's one of life's actual fighters, so maybe that gives it somewhat more weight... Peaceful as a backwoods Yet, ablaze inside. When you view as your middle You make certain to win. We should be quick as a flowing waterway With all the power of an extraordinary tropical storm With all the strength of a furious fire

Puzzling as the clouded side of the moon Still and quiet outwardly then, however with incredible power and strength within. Not driven by motivation or impulse, yet by more prominent reason. Never adapting to the desire of others and never surrendering whenever troubles arise. That is the champion soul.

Times You Were Not a Champion

You likely don't live on the front line and you presumably ideally won't ever have to see battle (albeit this book will guarantee that you are prepared on the off chance that you at any point do).

However, there are a lot of ways that the fighter outlook will apply in your everyday life too and a lot of chances to show the stuff to be a hero.

Maybe the simplest method for thinking about this is to take a gander at that multitude of times that you weren't a hero in your life. These are the times when your apprehension, your annoyance or your absence of inspiration and determination got the better of you.

Think about this:

•   You get up toward the beginning of the day and understand your number one shirt is torn, you use the remainder of the day furious with everybody, scowling and not focusing on your work. This tiny burden has destroyed your capacity to remain useful and it has caused others to feel awful.

• It's pouring out so you cancel your arrangements to visit your companion not too far off, who you know was anticipating the party.

• You're attempting to get in shape yet you're falling short on energy thus you eat an enormous piece of cake.

• A companion swoons at a party and on second thought of keeping mentally collected and following a right convention to ensure they're OK, you rather get in a fold, shout at everybody and exacerbate the situation.

• Your manager needs you to finish a task before you return home. You despise remaining later and you're feeling tired so you rush it and set forth not exactly your maximum effort.

• You have been telling companions for quite a long time that you will compose a book and that it is your fantasy to turn into a distributed writer. You return home and the main thing you do is pass out on the sofa and watch horrible television.

- You break a glass in the kitchen and when your accomplice asks who got it done, you fault your companion who was round recently.

- You get into an actual fight with somebody in the road and take off - passing on your companions or family to manage the risk all alone.

- You are getting onto a train and on second thought of letting the old woman on before you, you push ahead.

- Your companions are peer constraining you into partaking in weed and blaming you for not being entertaining. Partaking in weed is something you care very little about in this speculative circumstance yet you let yourself get talked into it because of a paranoid fear of seeming weak.

- You are cheerfully hitched when an alluring lady/man takes their action on you. You surrender to your transient motivation and you lay down with them, actually destroying your relationship with your accomplice as well as your kids too.

- You are despondent in your relationship or work however you stay in it since you don't have the heart to tell the individual or you are excessively scared of what the future could bring.

A portion of these models are more limit than others. Obviously, there is a major distinction between eating frozen yogurt when you truly shouldn't and being influenced by can't stand discourse! What's more, at times losing your cool is ordinary. In any case, while these focuses could in general appear to be altogether different, they basically come from exactly the same thing: shortcoming.

Shortcoming is many times the wellspring of our concerns and even of insidiousness. Shortcoming implies yielding to things we realize aren't correct, or rationalizing and putting off our objectives. Presently how about we take a gander at how somebody solid could move toward similar issues:

•   You get up toward the beginning of the day and understand your #1 shirt is torn. You shrug and wear something different, perceiving this is a tiny issue when it's all said and done!

•   It's pouring out and you don't want to go out. Be that as it may, you know it's the correct thing to do, so you man up and you go.

•   You're attempting to get more fit however you're coming up short on energy. You dig profound, track down that fire inside and go to the exercise center.

- A companion swoons at a party and you resist the urge to panic, cool and gathered. You allot responsibilities to individuals and check they're OK.

- Your manager needs you to finish a task before you return home. You dislike remaining later and you're feeling tired however you complete the work actually surprisingly well by the by. You address your manager about not setting you in that position once more.

- You have been telling companions for a really long time that you will compose a book and that it is your fantasy to turn into a distributed writer. You return home and take steps to compose two pages every evening.

- You break a glass in the kitchen and when your accomplice asks who got it done, you own up and confront the results.

- You get into an actual quarrel with somebody in the road. You ensure your loved ones are protected while attempting to quiet the circumstance overall quite well.

- You are getting onto a train and you generally stop to let the old woman on first. Also, the elderly person. Also, anybody who was there first.

• Your companions are peer forcing you into partaking in weed and blaming you for not being enjoyable. Assuming you need to, you do it. In the event that you don't, you don't.

• You are cheerfully hitched when an alluring lady/man takes their action on you. You have control of your sentiments so you turn them down.

• You are despondent in your relationship or work so you examine that misery with the other party and search for ways of advancing the circumstance. That could mean getting another line of work or cutting off the friendship yet it is superior to dawdling.

The champion is intellectually and genuinely impressive and this permits them to adhere to their implicit set of principles and to pursue their vision for a superior future - rather than doing what encourages them temporarily.

Eventually, this prompts a lot more prominent bliss, a lot more prominent harmony and a lot more noteworthy pride. As far as you might be concerned, however for every one of people around you.

CHAPTER 3

The Fire Inside

That line, the 'fire inside' is one that talks incredible volumes about the hero outlook. Also, it brings to mind verses from another melody: 'Hearts Ablaze' by the (brilliant) band Survivor.

An extraordinary line from that tune goes:

> In the fighter's code, there's no acquiescence

> However his body says stop, his soul cries: "Never!"

Anyway, what is this educating us concerning the champion mindset? Straightforward: fighters don't surrender and they don't yield. (I likewise partake in Vegeta's line: you might have attacked my brain and body however there's one thing a Saiyan generally keeps... his pride!)

So how would you acquire this sort of iron will and assurance? How would you foster the relentless capacity to never surrender?

It begins by understanding what you need to accomplish and by having your very own bunch standards.

To utilize one more statement, Alice Cooper and Xzibit sang:

On the off potential for success that you don't have for something, you will succumb to anything

Also, this is totally evident. Assuming you have no particular objective and no arrangement of values that is altogether your own, then how might you be supposed to adhere inflexibly to those qualities?

On the off chance that you haven't characterized what your identity is, what you're about and what is essential to you, then obviously getting enticed by great food, terrible television or other 'simple options will be simple'. Obviously, it will be simple for you to be influenced by the impact and the legislative issues of others.

Besides, having an objective will give you the inspiration and the energy to get up and pursue the things you are really amped up for.

Contemplate somebody like Arnold Schwarzenegger or Dwayne Johnson. These are individuals who have gotten inconceivable things done and part of the justification for that is without a doubt their apparently unending energy. Their capacity to get up each and every day and understand what they need to do.

Might you at any point envision seeing the Stone look drained and crestfallen? Have you at any point seen Arnold Schwarzenegger look apathetic or exhausted?

These individuals have resolute energy yet it comes from a dream and an objective. Thus it is with every one of the most achieved individuals over the entire course of time.

Arnie expressed this of his deep longing and how it drove him to achieve his objectives:

With my craving and drive, I certainly wasn't typical. Ordinary individuals can be content with a normal life. I was unique. I felt there was something else to life besides trudging through an ordinary presence... I have forever been dazzled by accounts of significance and power. I needed to accomplish something uniquely great, to be perceived as the best. I saw weight training as the vehicle that would take me to the top, and I set all my focus on it.

The fact is: understanding what you need from life will fuel you with energy, whether that needing's best for your family, needing to accomplish imaginative achievements, needing to arrive at a specific point in your vocation... and so on.

Ponder another parent. Guardians have apparently interminable energy and will forfeit their rest, their funds and their joy to take care of their kids. They can achieve anything since they have found an option that could be more significant than themselves.

A parent's affection will give them that fighter's mentality however you can't depend on only that. To achieve the most and to construct the best world for your loved ones, you additionally need something naturally rousing to you. All in all, you really want a reason and an objective that doesn't depend on any other person - so that in any event, when nobody needs you, you actually have the solidarity to haul yourself up and to deny interruptions and pointless longings.

When you have your objective, you will track down an energy. Furthermore, when you have an enthusiasm you will find that you have interminable energy and drive and that you even talk with additional conviction and more prominent mystique.

Did you had any idea that we gesture more when we talk about something that we're enthusiastic about? That is on the grounds that we are currently talking with our whole bodies - our non-verbal communication is consistent with what we are talking about.

Also, did you had any idea about that when individuals see us talk in like that, they really rate us as more charming? Really moving? What's more, better pioneers?

At the point when we truly have faith in what we are talking about, we will be more proficient at getting others to trust it. This is the means by which developments are begun and this makes us undeniably more appealing and attractive.

Also, with your objective and your goal, you can all the more likely decide and to keep away from superfluous interruptions. You will be more conclusive and you will be more amazing. Why? Since you can think about each choice through the accompanying focal point: 'does this assist me with accomplishing my objectives'? In the event that the response is no, you accomplish something different.

What vocation way would it be a good idea for you to take? The one that assists you with accomplishing your overall objectives. What party would it be a good idea for you to decide in favor of? The one that assists you with satisfying your vision.

Objectives and the Champions

The mark of the objective is to have something more significant than yourself - something that would definitely merit battling for.

All this resolve is something key to the brain research of history's most noteworthy fighters, however it took a totally different structure. All things considered, you had your samurai and your knights. A samurai's preparation went to incredible measures to guarantee their faithfulness to a 'shogun' (an expert samurai). They might want to pass on for their shogun, similarly as a ruler's knight might want to bite the dust for lord and for country.

Today however, this is risky reasoning. We are too mindful that our lawmakers are defective and we've perceived how indiscriminately following a pioneer or a bunch of convictions can prompt horrendous monstrosities.

Along these lines, what we want to do rather is to make our own arrangement of values and standards. Guidelines for effective living and an objective or a dream to take a stab at. This can change yet we should never allow others to compel us to act against our code.

Sadly, there is no impartially 'right' method for moving toward life. We don't have any idea why reality exists, what is sitting tight for us on the opposite side (on the off chance that anything) or what the importance of life is. In this manner, it ultimately depends on every one of us to make our own specific manner by evaluating our own qualities, standards and life affirming guidelines.

Tracking down Your Objective

Thus, let us start with finding an objective, an option that could be more significant than yourself to endeavor toward. A reason that you will be an instrument in achieving.

So this could imply that you set about influencing the world to improve things. Perhaps you need to stop world hunger, perhaps you need to assist with dialing back an unnatural weather change, or maybe you are keen on turning into a hero or a performer. Perhaps you simply need to get rich.

No objective is 'off-base', it is basically having an objective and something to be energetic about that will give you the fuel and the fire to continue to go regardless.

Objectives start with dreams. So picture the manner in which you maintain that life should be 5 or 10 years for the present. Picture where you are, what your environmental elements are, who you are with, what you've achieved. This ought to be a dream that makes you invigorated and empowered - your ideal life. For motivation, consider the times in your day to day existence you were most joyful, consider what you needed to be as a kid and picture a portion of your good examples and what you can maybe gain from them.

This is the very thing you will picture to drive yourself toward change and toward significance. This is the thing will get you up toward the beginning of the day. And afterward additionally, you will structure yourself objectives - more modest, more quantifiable advances that will assist you with arriving at that point.

Making Your Own Overarching set of rules On top of this, you will fabricate your own set of rules. What you would call what you view as 'living great' and 'making the best choice'.

Once more, this doesn't need to be your customary arrangement of rules. It is possible that you disagree for certain parts of the law. A few notable rationalists are known for sees that wanderer from traditional thoughts regarding morals and profound quality.

Take Ayn Rand for instance, who accepted that profound quality comes from what makes themmost joyful. She said:

Man has no programmed code of endurance... . His faculties don't tell him naturally what is great for him or wickedness, what will help his life or imperil it, what objectives he ought to seek after and what means will accomplish them, what esteems his life relies upon, strategy its expectation. Man should pick his activities, values and objectives by the norm of that which is legitimate to man - to accomplish, keep up with, satisfy and partake in that extreme worth, that end in itself, which is his own life.

She accepted that singular profound quality ought to be founded on what makes that individual most joyful. That implies dealing with things that you love, working on yourself and safeguarding the ones you care about... who thus make you more joyful.

Rand would recommend that we ought to take care of our families and our friends and family, seek after our interests and our self-advancement and that way add to society.

Anything you trust your code to be, you get it on paper and afterward resolve to adhere to that code. Like that, you will not be convinced by others, you will actually want to battle for your qualities and individuals will know where they stand with you.

All things considered, you likewise ought not be reluctant to develop and adjust your thoughts after some time. For that reason it is so essential to continue perusing and continue to learn. Stay up with the latest with legislative issues and what is happening on the planet, read way of thinking and reevaluate your qualities.

There is no worth in adhering to one bunch of objectives or standards endlessly and declining to readdress them, as eventually this turns into a 'lie' as much as some other You shouldn't cast a ballot a specific way since you have consistently casted a ballot a specific way. Furthermore, you ought not be hesitant to rethink the way that you feel about specific parts of your code.

The fact of the matter is that you won't break your general set of principles while it exists. You have norms to maintain and the basic demonstration of maintaining them will make you a more grounded, bolder and more great person.

CHAPTER 4

Defeating Dread

At the point when we consider the original hero, we will more than likely make certain to consider somebody that is daring, bold and apparently intrepid. This is the sort of individual that will stroll into the line of fire. That will stand in opposition to shamefulness, that will take on foes that are a lot more prominent than them.

In our own lives, there are no genuine mythical beasts to kill. Rather, they take on numerous different structures, whether they be ailment, whether they be obligation, or whether they be the battle of going to the rec center consistently…

Step by step instructions to Utilize 'Dread Setting'

In the event that you love perusing self improvement writing, odds are sooner or later you will have recorded your objectives. This is the sort of thing that pretty much every master appears to prompt and that many case can assist you with achieving your fantasies by better characterizing and imagining them.

In any case, in Tim Ferriss' 4 Hour Long week of work this guidance is flipped completely around fairly. While Tim doesn't be guaranteed to disapprove of objective setting per-say, he additionally suggests doing basically the inverse by 'dread setting'. Furthermore, he guarantees it can do significantly more than objective setting with regards to understanding your points and getting more from life...

What is Dread Setting?

The overall thought behind dread setting is that you're characterizing the feelings of trepidation that are keeping you down so you can confront them. By and large Tim proposes that in the wake of doing this you'll observe that your feelings of dread are quite unwarranted and accordingly will push ahead and past them. Regularly our apprehensions are of 'irreversible' adverse results, yet really these are more uncommon than you could naturally suspect...

So what you do is to record the most awful potential results for doing anything it is you need to do, and afterward record every one of the manners in which you'd adapt to the circumstance or perhaps turn around it.

A Model: Changing Profession

How about we accept changing profession for instance. This is the sort of thing that a many individuals need to do, however feel kept down by dread of possible repercussions. By characterizing those fears however, you can limit their intensity.

So in the event that you planned to record the absolute worst results for evolving professions, it could well look something like this:

- I could relinquish my position just to neglect to secure another position

- I may not be able to pay the home loan and in this way be compelled to move home

- This could agitate my accomplice such a lot of they leave me

- I could land the position I assume I need and figure out I disdain it more than my last work

- I could apply to different positions just to get dismissed by everybody and wind up harming my inner self.

These are genuine worries, yet presently assuming you ponder every one of the manners in which you can oversee risk and decrease the effects of those adverse results you'll find your feelings of dread aren't exactly established...

- I can search for occupations without passing on my present place of employment to keep away from the gamble of joblessness. Nobody needs to be aware.

- This will likewise be significantly less wild according to my accomplice.

- On the other hand I could address my manager about my concerns and check whether there are different situations inside my association.

- In the event that I truly do wind up unemployed I could continuously address my old supervisor about landing my position back/work in a grocery store while I search for other work/work for Father/live off of reserve funds for two or three months/move back home with the guardians!

• On the off chance that my accomplice leaves me for attempting to become more joyful, I want to rethink that relationship

• On the off chance that I could do without the gig I find next then I will have good expectations about work hunting in the future in future.

• Assuming I battle to go anyplace I can deal with my meeting procedure/work on my CV/look for profession direction. At any rate, which will all be valuable encounters.

As you can see then, the exceptionally most terrible situation is presumably not quite as terrible as it appears - it might simply mean living out of reserve funds for some time or making a little stride in reverse to take two advances. Moreover, as there are such countless ways of limiting the gamble of things turning out badly, it's very far-fetched you'll wind up in those positions in any case.

In The 4 Hour Long week of work Tim likewise offers another piece of guidance that I feel is exceptionally significant here: don't request consent, request pardoning. Take that mentality and diagram your feelings of dread and you're on target to a more joyful rendition of yourself as well as to achieving considerably more.

Emotionlessness and the Fighter Mentality

Tim Ferriss' thoughts could appear to be remarkable however, he says himself that he is enlivened by old way of thinking and explicitly, by the thoughts of the antiquated Stoics. Apathy is a school of reasoning that dates as far as possible back to the third Century BC. Its standards were founded and practiced by verifiable characters like Epictetus, Seneca and Marcus Aurelius.

What's more, in numerous ways, Emotionlessness was an early way to deal with a 'champion mentality'. Everything really revolved around mental strength and about figuring out how to expect and afterward live with things veering off-track. As a matter of fact, a considerable lot of us portray somebody who is daring and gutsy as being unemotional.

All in all, what definitively does it include?

The Force of Cynicism

On the off chance that we let somebody know that we don't think things will work out as we trusted, then they'll frequently let us know that we should be 'more hopeful'.

There's even a tune that tells us to 'complement the positive' and 'kill the negative'. The overall agreement is clear: being positive is something to be thankful for and being something besides sure is unsatisfactory.

However, is this actually the most ideal way for us to move toward our concerns? Or on the other hand is it maybe quite harming to continually be dazed by confidence? Does it leave us powerless against dissatisfaction and possibly effectively surprised? Is supposed life to be continually 'daylight and rainbows' the exact inverse of a hero outlook?

Couldn't a fighter acknowledge and embrace the way that life will be hard? And afterward harden themselves up to manage it?

That is the view held by stoics in any event and when you dive into the way of thinking a bit, you could find that they really make a generally excellent case for negativity.

The Focal Thoughts of Aloofness

The overall substance of emotionlessness isn't to attempt to 'close out' cynicism and imagine that terrible things don't occur yet rather to embrace it and even to involve it as a device. Trust, as per the stoics, is the adversary, unequivocally on the grounds that it implies we're caught off guard for things turning out badly and we're probably going to be disheartened.

All things considered, emotionlessness advocates the idea of dirty authenticity - of perceiving the pessimistic parts of life and tolerating that a ton of what happens is beyond our control and is presumably not going to be extremely lovely!

Involving Aloofness in Your Own Life

This probably won't seem like an especially supportive position to take on things, however at that point that is on the grounds that the greater part of us are exceptionally prepared into just tolerating positive perspectives. This is the overall vanity of endless self improvement guides and, surprisingly, Hollywood movies. Think beyond practical boundaries and you can get what you need! It's basically the main thrust behind free enterprise, truth be told.

In any case, the Stoics adopt the contrary strategy. They plan for the tempest. They figure out how to appreciate life in any event, when things aren't turning out well for them and they perceive difficulty aschallenge and a chance for development.

When you carry on with life feeling qualified for everything turning out well for you, how might you expected to be content? Furthermore, how might you be supposed to confront difficulties that are really troublesome?

So how does dismissing this ceaseless energy help? How would you basically apply aloofness in your own life? Negative Perception One idea from apathy is something many refer to as 'negative perception' - the possibility that you picture your feelings of trepidation instead of your objectives. Rather than envisioning things going impeccably to design, all things considered, picture things best case scenario. Envision how your arrangements can fall flat and picture what life would resemble on the off chance that every one of your most awful feelings of dread materialized.

What this does is to initially assist you with planning for those most pessimistic scenario situations. When you understand what your apprehensions really resemble, you can then ponder how you would adapt in that situation. Frequently, you'll observe that this most dire outcome imaginable isn't generally so awful as you from the start figured it would be. What's more, in different cases, you'll find that you can really track down ways of adapting to that.

This eliminates fears that could somehow or another keep you down and implies that you're not aimlessly disregarding what might actually turn out badly.

On the off chance that this sounds natural, that is on the grounds that exactly a similar idea assisted Tim Ferriss with concocting his Trepidation Setting method.

Be Happy With the Scantiest and Least expensive Toll In one of his letters to Lucilius, Seneca said:

Put away a specific number of days, during which you will be happy with the scantiest and least expensive passage, with coarse and unpleasant dress, telling yourself the while: is this the condition that I dreaded?

The overall thought here, is that you shouldn't just picture your most dire outcome imaginable, yet additionally take a stab at living it. That could mean enduring seven days living off of least compensation, it could try and mean dozing unpleasant.

Regardless, this shows you not just that you can deal with your most obviously awful feelings of dread - and hence have less motivation to be apprehensive - yet in addition that you really don't require material belongings to be content.

This is really something vital to develop. It takes extraordinary discipline to leave behind your assets and possessions yet the outcome is independence from dread and furthermore from numerous actual limitations. In the event that you are burdened by assets and possessions, you can not move home unreservedly. You will invest a great deal of energy cleaning and taking care of things that don't assist you with facilitating your objectives. Furthermore, eventually, you will have substantially more to fear.

The more you own, the more you need to lose. This makes a feeling of dread.

Thus, attempt to clean up and carry on with a more focused and moderate life. In any event, figure out how to segregate yourself from actual belongings and recall that they are without a doubt 'just things'. They are a necessary evil and on the off chance that you should forfeit them, so be it.

Selling your widescreen television or turning down a vacation to take care of obligation or pay for your youngster's educational cost - those are hero like decisions. Wear Terrible Garments...

Another exemplary emotionless move is to wear 'revolting' garments to show yourself not to be embarrassed. Individuals could gaze at you, yet this will basically instruct you that it doesn't make any difference whatsoever others' thought process - just your thought process.

This is a significant part of the champion outlook: tending to think about others' thought process makes you helpless against peer pressure and to vanity. Some of the time, to do what should be finished, you should forfeit your standing.

Similarly as in our model about conceding that you broke the jar... Anticipate Just horrible Stoics contend that we revile when we're furious and that this outrage is our own faltering - our own ineptitude.

Ponder the last time you swore with outrage. Odds are it was not on the grounds that it down-poured or in light of the fact that you found you were under water. More probable, it was since you dropped something on your toe, or on the grounds that you broke your #1 belonging.

The fact is that the resentment comes from the astonishment, not the mistake. You don't swear when it downpours since you realize that downpour is plausible.

Consequently, in the event that you are furious, this recommends that you didn't expect whatever happened to you and this is apparently your own shortcoming. Assuming you acknowledge that awful things occur and on the off chance that you acknowledge that occasionally things will not go to design, then you will have compelling reason should be irate - in light of the fact that you will have represented it and arranged intellectually for it.

Presently, when your accomplice undermines you, or when a specialist co-op doesn't convey a decent help, you will consider it being basically a piece of life - very much like the downpour.

Control Your Response

Aloofness implies submitting to the way that you have inadequate to zero influence over the real world. And yet, it additionally implies taking comfort in the information that these external variables can't hurt you - just your response can.

You have no control over what befalls you except for you have some control over what you think about that occasion and your own translation of it. Being intellectually ready for things that could turn out badly is one genuine illustration of this in real life. Similarly however, you could likewise basically choose not to allow things to influence you - to make a stride back from

them and to manage the outcomes instead of whipping against things that you can't change. This is the sort of thing we'll address all the more intently in forthcoming sections: care and the capacity to conclude how you need to respond to the things happening around you.

Yet, essentially by recollecting that extreme things occur and you must manage them, you ought to find you can I really believe that Rough Balboa is one of the extraordinary current stoics - and one of his later well known expressions sums up the thoughts of Seneca and Marcus Aurelius impeccably:

The world ain't all daylight and rainbows. It's an exceptionally mean and frightful spot... also, it doesn't matter at all to me how extreme you are, it will beat you to your knees and keep you there forever, assuming you let it. You, me or no one, will hit as hard as life. Yet, ain't about how hard you hit... It's about how hard you can get hit, and continue to push ahead... the amount you can take, and continue to push ahead. That is the way winning is finished.

Here is a statement from fiction a book I composed quite a while prior. This line was spoken by a careless person in the story and was never intended to convey a lot of weight. However, I found that as I mulled over everything, it was quite obvious:

Those that dread passing, dread life.

The facts really confirm that on the off chance that you carry on with life in feeling of dread toward death, you will be forever mindful. You won't face challenges and you won't carry on with life to its fullest thus.

Anyway, what is the arrangement? Would we put passing 'out of our care'. No: it would be smarter to find a sense of peace with it and in emotionless design, just embrace it as a situation. Also, this mirrors the way that the Samurai would move toward their lives as well. Here is a statement from Edo samurai DaidojiYuzan, which can be found in the book Code of the Samurai:

One who is a samurai must before everything remember continually... the way that he needs to pass on. In the event that he is dependably aware of this, he will actually want to live as per the ways of devotion and obedient obligation, will stay away from hordes of wrongs and difficulties, keep himself liberated from illness and disaster and besides partake in a long life. He will likewise be a fine character with numerous commendable characteristics. For presence is fleeting as the dew of night, and the hoarfrost of morning, and especially unsure is the existence of the hero...

Recall your objectives and your vision. Pursue them. Adhere to your code. Attempt to have an effect and spotlight on what you abandon. That could mean safeguarding your family in any event, when it implies seriously endangering yourself, or it could mean taking risks to pursue a greater objective.

CHAPTER 5

Development Mentality

In the last section, we took a gander at the significance of conquering dread - in any event, beating an apprehension about death.

Furthermore, comparatively, it is similarly critical to be awkward and to encounter modest quantities of difficulty. How might you shed pounds assuming that you fear abstaining from excessive food intake? How might you hope to advance in your vocation assuming that you avoid difficult work?

Be that as it may, this is the truth for the majority of us. We are essentially reluctant to do things we would rather not do, or to tolerate difficult situations. We have become really frail and it is eventually making us troubled.

Why We Have Become Frail

Think about your canine and contrast them with a wolf (in the event that you don't possess a canine, consider one you know). Check the distinctions out.

Your canine may be adoring, faithful and tomfoolery however it is altogether reliant upon you. It wouldn't endure a day in the wild and it's surely not a fighter like the wolf is.

No difference either way. Since it has been trained.

What's more, that my companion, is your concern too.

We have become tamed as well as become lethargic, ruined and excessively reveled. In present day culture, everything is dispensable, everything comes effectively and we never need to stand by.

Hungry? Request a focal point. It will be with you in a short time and it will be loaded with salt and sugar so you feel a surge of remuneration chemicals.

Horny? Observe some pornography.

Exhausted? Turn on the television and chuckle at somebody falling over.

Need data? Simply ask Siri.

Need to get into better shape? Naah, that appears to be a ton of exertion.

Being so continually enjoyed anything we desire implies that we find it harder than at any other time to invest energy when it is required. How could we invest energy when we can have so a lot, with such ease?

What's more, similarly, when we are accustomed to getting anything we desire, we feel totally troubled when the shower doesn't warm up as expected.

Furthermore, consider this: in the wild, you would have just had cold water to wash in. Eating would have required hunting or scavenging in the downpour while staying away from hunters. You could be such a great deal more grounded thus a lot harder - intellectually and genuinely. Yet, as we are, we're fat, sluggish and falling short on inspiration.

The most effective method to Get Intense

So considering that, how would you approach getting intense?

The principal thing you want to do, is to take a stab at living with less. We examined this generally in our post on Emotionlessness, yet voyaging is a fabulous method for achieving the champion mentality. That implies voyaging and remaining in lodgings, not booking lodgings the prior night, just taking a couple of garments.

I have been on a couple of excursions like this myself. I went out traveling around Europe and took just a rucksack to squeeze by. I lay at a train station in Poland in the snow, unfit to peruse the signs (in spite of my Clean legacy) and not knowing when the following train would come. Or then again even where I was! This was before information meandering or 3G, so that was not feasible as well.

Then I tracked down a little bistro and figured out how to arrange some tea - with milk as opposed to with a lemon as the Clean for the most part drink it.

Guess what? I felt really delight drinking from that polystyrene cup. I valued the tea so much since it had been for such a long time and in light of the fact that I was so cold.

Today, I frequently request my tea in polystyrene cups when it's a choice since it sends me back to that second.

Furthermore, this is the thing you understand when you drive yourself to manage without: you discover that the easily overlooked details can give you a ton of pleasure. That there is prize and satisfaction to be tracked down in each second. You needn't bother with all that to entirely go.

What's more, as a matter of fact, when things turn out badly, it makes stories and assists you with developing further.

Development Outlook

What's more, that is a central issue in fact: to keep a development outlook consistently. Each challenge that comes your direction is an opportunity to get more grounded, more intelligent and better. By managing these difficulties, your life has more noteworthy reason (life is futile when it is simple) and you turn out to be better prepared to take on comparative difficulties in future.

Thus, the following time you end up under water, rather than allowing it to overcome you, rather consider it to be a test. How might you bring in the cash you really want to receive in return? How might you turn out to be better?

Try not to flounder in pressure or tension - that helps nobody. Consider it to be an opportunity to develop and to forestall this reoccurring and do whatever it takes. Try not to stress over how it appears to other people, don't fault yourself for allowing yourself to get into that particular situation previously.

Simply make a move. Also, gain from it. You were not sufficient previously yet presently you will be better.

As a matter of fact, development and challenge are things that the cerebrum is really wired for. We flourish when we are tested intellectually and actually and this outcomes in the creation of chemicals like dopamine, mind determined neurotrophic element and more that keep us focussed and that assist with safeguarding our cerebrums into advanced age.

Besides the fact that you welcome should the difficulties that come, you ought to search them out. During 'seasons of harmony', you ought to plan for the fight to come by getting the hang of (understanding books, embracing new abilities) and via preparing your body.

CHAPTER 6

Apparatuses for Development and Versatility

We've rambled about how the champion mindset involves greater versatility, more prominent persistence, smoothness and strength. Yet, the genuine inquiry is the manner by which you arrive at that point. How might you acquire that champion mentality?

Ideally at this point you comprehend what the fighter mentality is and what it implies in a more extensive setting yet how might you conquer your shortcomings and your desire to eat cake, to unwind and to take the simple choices?

The following are a couple of incredible assets that will assist you with developing and become further.

Contemplation

Contemplation is an outright unquestionable necessity for a cutting edge fighter. This is one of the absolute most incredible assets for changing your outlook and for giving you the versatility, solidness and feeling of quiet you want to pick how you respond to your feelings and sentiments.

Reflection is just the act of concentrating your psyche, of discharging your mind of contemplations and of figuring out how to try not to divert thoughts and motivations. This takes extraordinary mental discipline and in that sense, an ideal device for preparing discipline. Truly, focus is discipline!

In addition, is that contemplation trains you to divert from your tensions, your inclinations and your longings. Careful reflection trains you to allow your contemplations to float by without influencing you, while supernatural clears your psyche completely.

This is an extraordinary method for quieting your physiology when pushed or stirred and to assume back command of your viewpoints and activities. The people who reflect are more settled and less handily bothered and this liberates them to act in the most thought of and powerful way.

At last, contemplation is an extraordinary method for re-energizing your batteries and acquire energy, which thusly permits you to execute your arrangements.

Seinfeld credits contemplation with furnishing him with perpetual energy. He says that he would almost certainly still be doing the show and wouldn't have worn out, had he currently consistently rehearsed TM (supernatural reflection):

I'll get up at 6 a.m. My children become up around 6:45 a.m. Thus I do the TM before anyone gets. Also, how can it feel? It doesn't feel like anything. I don't figure out it. Be that as it may, here's the distinction. At 1 p.m. that day, my head doesn't raise a ruckus around town like it used to. That is the distinction. On the off chance that I didn't do TM that morning and I'm working, then, at that point, by 1 p.m. I'm shot, and I think the vast majority are. What's more, presently, at 1 o'clock, I'm feeling quite a bit better. I simply sail as the day progressed, and afterward I have my second TM at 3 p.m. or on the other hand 4 p.m.

Right Relaxing

Another apparatus you can use to recover and enter the hero mentality voluntarily is right relaxing. This implies stomach breathing, breathing from your stomach first and taking full breaths. This quiets your sensory system and places you into the rest and review express, it's the ideal method for conquering uneasiness.

Cold Showers

Cold showers increment your digestion, they assist you with delivering more testosterone and they cause a flood or adrenaline. They can really fortify your resistant framework as well. As such, they're great for yourself and an extraordinary method for beginning your day.

And yet, they hurt and they suck. This is a horrendous shock to the framework and it's the last thing you need to do.

Which is definitively why it is great for your champion preparation. Cleaning up requires mind blowing mental discipline and on the off chance that you can compel yourself to do this consistently, then you can accomplish pretty much anything.

What's more, as a great truth, Hugh Jackman said that he involved cold showers as a method for getting into the brain of Wolverine for the X-Men motion pictures. Presently there's a champion that you could stand to be more similar to!

Strength Preparing and Hand to hand fighting

What do every one of the champions through history share practically speaking?

They are not simply intellectually intense - albeit that has been the focal point of this book - they are additionally actually extreme. This is vital in light of the fact that actual sturdiness gives you the strength, the purpose and the ability to be certain and to persevere when you really do have to battle for your qualities.

It is significant where conceivable not to battle but rather really, being impressive actually will assist you with keeping away from the need to battle.

That, yet it will empower you to safeguard the ones you love.

What's more, both combative techniques and power lifting will assist you with developing while likewise imparting incredible self-control. To build your possibilities prevailing on your excursion, take up a military workmanship and try to head out to the rec center 3 or 4 times each week.

As Socrates said:

No man has the privilege to be a beginner in the question of actual preparation. It is a disgrace for a man to become old without seeing the excellence and strength of which his body is skilled.

CHAPTER 7

Applying Exemplary Hero Standards to Business and Life

I generally thought it was something of style proclamation for finance managers and ladies to convey duplicates of The Craft of Battle by Sun Tsu. I comprehended their case that it was pertinent to business methodology and that a large number of the thoughts are as yet significant, however everything appeared to be a bit whimsical to me. More like vanity and presenting! How should 1,000 year-old composition truly be pertinent to the present universe of PCs and cell phones?

That was until I started to rehearse the fighter outlook and immediately understood that it really is exceptionally applicable. Without a doubt, it won't train you to utilize MSWord, yet as far as promoting, initiative and the administration of assets it is still exceptionally helpful. These thoughts and ideas are ageless and can be applied in practically boundless circumstances. Take a gander at it along these lines, on the off chance that the counsel is sufficient to assist you with winning conflicts with blades and bolts, then, at that point, definitely it can assist you with getting Bill from bookkeeping to quit griping.

In light of that I present the absolute best statements and examples from the book that you can take with you into the workplace and us to move more faithfulness and efficiency. Also, only just in case I've tossed in some Machiavelli; who composed The Sovereign as a guidance manual for an Italian ruler that would assist him with turning into a powerful ruler sometime in the not so distant future.

These are the two texts focused on authentic fighters and rulers but they are desired by business experts, relationship masters and that's just the beginning. This is the ideal illustration of why the fighter attitude is as yet pertinent today and you will see that the feelings in that reverberation a lot of what we have proactively examined.

Illustrations from the Specialty of War

There is No Example of a Country Profiting From Delayed Fighting

All in all, in the event that you are in conflict with a contender or a partner, a drawn out battle will just harm both of you. This is known as a 'pyrrhic triumph' - an expression that comes from another renowned verifiable fight. Toward the end regardless of whether you win, you will have harmed your

notoriety and squandered your assets so that you're left with only a Pyrrhic Triumph. Rather then, check whether you can't transform a rival into a partner and find a way that you both can benefit all things being equal.

Keep in mind, the fighter picks their fights astutely. The fighter outlook isn't tied in with being forceful and traditionalist. It is tied in with being ready, excusing and sufficiently strong to not have to make the slightest effort.

This then, at that point, makes sense of one more of Sun Tsu's statements: the preeminent specialty of war is to quell the foe without battling. This is exceptionally applicable to current heroes - more genuine now than at any other time.

Valuable open doors Increase As They Are Seized

Assuming you needed an illustration of how The Specialty of War can straightforwardly apply to business then this is all there is to it. To what lengths all the more impeccably might you at some point will go for this to portray the method involved with making ventures? You need to spend to gather!

Recollect how Arnie picked weight training as a way and a springboard to better progress? You can also pick shrewdly to yield extraordinary outcomes from basic beginning stages.

Know the foe and know yourself; in 100 fights you won't ever be in danger.

This is an undeniable one that rams home the significance of both exploring the market, and taking a gander at your own criticism to guarantee you are best ready to take on the opposition. In the event that you thought Sun Tsu just overlooks clear focuses however he proceeds to grow: When you are oblivious to the foe, yet know yourself, your possibilities winning or losing are equivalent. In the event that uninformed about both your adversary and yourself, you are sure in each fight to be in danger.

Beyond the workplace, we have proactively examined how realizing yourself will permit you to shape your own principles and your own objectives and goals.

The overall who propels without desiring notoriety and retreats without dreading shame, whose main idea is to safeguard his nation and do great help for his sovereign, is the gem of the realm.

This is the sort of worker you need - watch out for the people who bring an excess of self image to the work environment. This is the sort of worker you should be. Also, this impeccably repeats Seneca's perspectives on living with less prior on.

Keep in mind, for this situation you are not serving your nation or sovereign but rather the higher reason and values that you decided for yourself.

Successful heroes win first and afterward do battle, while crushed champions do battle first and afterward look to win.

Arranging is everything. Before you offer your item or administration for sale to the public your prosperity or disappointment is an inevitable end product - so ensure you've tried things out and investigated completely.

What's more, again this addresses the quiet and determined nature of the hero - the fighter doesn't rush in head-first, regardless of their command over their trepidation.

Illustrations From The Sovereign

Whosoever wants steady achievement should change his lead with the times.

This is especially critical to note on the off chance that you run a huge association and are at risk for becoming complacent. Be thinking one stride ahead consistently to stay away from a similar destiny as Kodak. This repeats the opinions we examined before as well, about being willing to change your standards and adjust where essential. In any case, this ought to come from the inside, not from without.

Men should be all around treated or squashed, on the grounds that they can vindicate themselves of lighter wounds, of additional serious ones they can't.

'Smashing' your adversaries and workers may not be energized in moral business (strangely Sun Tsu is considerably more conservative than Machiavelli) yet the fact of the matter is as yet substantial - don't make foes then, at that point, give them an opportunity to rest and recover.

Quite far, the hero ought to keep away from battle and conflict. They ought to try to satisfy everybody and track down the most commonly useful result.

Be that as it may, on the off chance that you truly do choose to take part in contest or battle, you should act with conclusion.

The astute man does without a moment's delay what the idiot does at last.

For example Time is cash and hesitation is a recipe for disappointment.

Business people are basically the individuals who comprehend that there is little distinction among obstruction and opportunity and can make both advantageous for them.

This is definitely surprisingly exacting. Opening a tin of beans without any problem: challenge or opportunity? This is like the thoughts we examined before about considering challenge to be an opportunity for development. Also, how insane is it to imagine that Machiavelli could have had such applicable and valuable guidance for current business visionaries.

However more verification that the champion attitude is ageless and similarly as significant today as ever previously. Anything can be drawn nearer as a hero.

I enthusiastically suggest perusing these books as a feature of your development and your excursion to turning into your best self. They have a place on each champion's understanding rundown.

CHAPTER 8

Decision: Taking a Harder Street

We're arriving at the finish of our excursion together now however yours is just start. Now is the ideal time to begin putting yourself out there, testing yourself, developing, taking on difficulties and choosing what means quite a bit to you. Now is the ideal time to quit worrying the little stuff, to stop the common luxuries and to embrace a really difficult and requesting life - on the grounds that that is where the worth comes from and that is the thing will make you incredible.

However, a fair warning before you go: this will be extreme.

You will find that occasionally, making the best choice and overlooking your profound reaction implies making statements individuals could do without.

Adhering to your standards will mean messing everything up.

Failing to remember how you look will lead you to in some cases be disregarded.

Failing to remember actual belongings will leave you some of the time feeling desperate.

In any case, assuming that you know yourself genuinely, assuming you know your objectives, you understand what you need and you know the standards you need to live by... then you will know the right activities and you ought to have the solidarity to do them.

Furthermore, that implies living with the outcomes.

Also, that is the last example I need to confer upon you: recognize the cold hard reality. Put yourself out there, face challenges and afterward face the flack that comes your direction. This all follows on from the examples on apathy, moderation and dread that we have proactively thought of. Yet, it is profoundly significant.

When you discover that occasionally you'll misunderstand things - and you acknowledge and figure out how to manage the result - you'll find that you become an additional definitive and more proficient person.

Individuals who are reluctant to settle on some unacceptable decision and who would rather not furious anybody will always be unable to decide. They'll constantly be vacillating and they will need conviction.

That is not you. You are a champion and that implies you really want to follow your own way and face the outcomes as a developed grown-up.

You will request pardoning and not authorization. Also, on the off chance that you don't get it? In any case, however long you have made the wisest decision by you, then, at that point, you continue onward.

You are the fighter.